YOUR GUIDE

BETTER

FOLLOWERSHIP

Discover the SECRETS to Becoming
More Effective Tomorrow
Than You Are Today

Volume 1, 4th Edition

TO

THE EFFECTIVENESS GUIDE

BY

EDWARD J. MURPHY

LEE O. LACY & JASON BOWNE

CAREER MAKER PUBLISHING

Copyright © 2012 by *THE CAREER PUBLISHING*

YOUR GUIDE TO BETTER FOLLOWERSHIP: Discover the SECRETS to Becoming More Effective Tomorrow Than You Are Today

Volume 1, 4th Edition, to *The Effectiveness Guide*

By EDWARD J. MURPHY, with LEE O. LACY & JASON BOWNE

Career Maker Publishing

10240 E. Tillman Avenue, Mesa, AZ 85212; 816.347.0591

ISBN-13: 978-1516873463; ISBN-10: 1516873467

BISAC: Business & Economics / Leadership / LU: 0718

For special orders, please email, ed.murphy77@gmail.com.

WHAT OTHER SAY ABOUT
The Effectiveness Guide

"I highly recommend The Effectiveness Guide as a text for new leaders and a review for seasoned leaders - as a reminder of what they should be doing. This book is unique because it's replete with valuable information that you can learn today and use tomorrow. If you want to be absolutely essential to any organization and become a better leader tomorrow than you are today, then this is for you."

- Dennis D. Cavin
Lieutenant General, US Army (Retired)
Vice President Army and Missile Defense Programs
Lockheed Martin, Corporate Business Development

"I wish to recommend The Effectiveness Guide because Ed Murphy just doesn't theorize; he draws on extensive organizational experience from many years of service in the military and from working in the private-sector. His keen insights and practical advice make this book required reading for anyone trying to negotiate the maze of organizational chaos."

- Lee Lacy
Assistant Professor
US Army Warfighter Course
Command and General Staff College

"The Effectiveness Guide will help you discover the qualities of effectiveness. It will also help you unlock your potential to direct and lead your team to success. Leadership is an art as well as a science. This book will help you master both the art and science of leadership. I highly recommend this guide."

- Lance Revo
Principal Engineering Design Specialist
Cyber Security at AREVA NP

I DEDICATE THIS BOOK

TO

My Grandson,

MICHAEL VINCENT PAUL

"My MVP"

"Mike, I won't be around during your lifetime. But if I were, I would tell you exactly what's in this book. That's why I wrote it. May it help you and your posterity find true joy and enhance the quality of your life. Make a difference in the lives of others by serving them, in some meaningful way, and you will be richly rewarded in life and in the next. Know that I am always with you! Much love always."

CONTENTS

Become More Effective Tomorrow Than You Are Today

PREFACE

I'm often asked, "What does the picture mean on the cover of your book?"

This picture is a metaphor of the dilemma young people face coming from high school or college into the world-of-work.

They're unprepared, do not have the right tools, the right motivation, nor any clue of what's most important to every employer on the planet.

The cover image shows a young man rowing a boat in the fog. If you  *look closer, you'll notice that the boat is too small for the person in it. You can tell because one side of the boat is dipping so low in the water that it's almost taking on water. You can also tell that he has little experience in a boat because the other side of the boat is way out of the water because his weight is not evenly distributed. He is also rowing in dense fog. He cannot see where he's going. The further he gets from shore, he cannot turn around and head back because he has no idea from which direction he came. Finally, since he's not wearing a flotation device, he's assuming he won't have to swim. You know where assumptions take you, right? He is totally unprepared. He didn't plan his trip, nor is he prepared to deal with the consequences of what lies ahead. He is, or will soon be, lost and at the mercy of nature.*

Such is the fate of young workers today.

In today's job market there's a huge skills gap between graduation and the first day on the job. As a result, young people lack the job skills needed to "hit-the-ground-running" and find themselves in dead-end, menial, minimum-wage jobs, trading time for money just to put food on the table.

How do I know that? I know it because I've spent 20+ years of my life as an executive coach, working with hundreds of business executives and small business owners, seeking the answer to this simple question:

Why are some people more effective than others?

What do they think, say, and do that made them more effective?

During that time, I was privileged to work with some of the most exceptional men and women in America. Through their example, I learned the true definition of effectiveness by documenting what they did, how they did it, and most importantly, how they made people feel. What you'll find here is the result of my years of research.

Today, my purpose in life is to help you navigate the world-of-work, maximize their true career potential, and become more effective and successful at work and in life.

ENJOY!

INTRODUCTION

"Keep interested in your career, however humble;
it is a real possession in the changing fortunes of time.
- Desiderata

How effective are you at work? Would your employer agree? What are you doing every day to become more effective? These are the questions we'll be addressing as we explore how you can become more effective tomorrow than you are today.

This book is about *Followership, your ability to consistently produce excellent results by supporting your employer in the accomplishment of his goals.*

Followership is one of the *10 Core Competencies of Effectiveness:*

Followership, Delegating, Planning, Organizing, Communicating, Problem-Solving, Awareness, Training, Motivating, and Character.

Volume 1: *Your Guide to Better Followership*, is one in a series of 10 books that comprise *The Effectiveness Guide,* which was created to provide you with the best-in-class knowledge, wisdom, and advice on how you can become more effective at work and in life. It contains over 1000 actionable Tactics, Techniques, and Tools (or best practices) used every day by the most effective people in their field and have proven reliable in helping others to maximize their true career potential.

In a 21st-century world of business, the best companies, the ones who make it to the top in their industry, are thriving because they're breaking all the traditional rules and stereotypes of conventional leadership. Positions, titles, and organizational charts are meaningless.

I know this to be true because I've spent 20 years of my life as an executive coach working with hundreds of business executives and small business owners, seeking the answer to this simple question,

Why are some people more effective than others?

What do they think, say, and do that made them more effective?

Here, I was privileged to work with some of the most exceptional men and women in America, learning the true meaning of effectiveness by documenting what they did, how they did it, and most importantly, how they made others feel. I found that effective people had one thing in common.

They were able to influence the actions of others by how well they applied the 10 Core Competencies of Effectiveness.

I also learned why most businesses today are struggling.

First, employers today are still relying on traditional development practices, which are stunting the growth of many young leaders. They're still asking the wrong questions and using the same old lame metrics to measure success, which isn't working as expected. Traditional assessments like 360 surveys or outdated performance criteria give false positives, lulling people into thinking they're more prepared than they are.

Second, there's a huge skills gap between graduation and the first day on the job. As a result, new employees lack the job skills needed to "hit the ground running" and find themselves in dead-end, menial, minimum-wage jobs, trading time for money just to put food on the table.

Third, most employees have no program for professional development and become complacent hoping that their past accomplishments are good enough, and no longer strive to improve their skills. They wait for their employer to tell them that they have a weakness before they do anything to improve themselves. There's no motivation to empower them to "Be All They Can Be."

And, finally, employers, especially small business owners, lack the time or resources to train their employees. Worse yet, large corporations today aren't willing to invest in training their employees until they have a proven track-record.

It's clear to me that the leadership and management wisdom used for years doesn't work anymore and is failing us in several critical areas. There's got to be a better way. Well, there is, and it's called effectiveness.

Effectiveness is your ability to consistently produce excellent results.

When assessing effectiveness, no one cares how much experience you have, how hard or how long you work, where you went to college, or what companies you worked for; all that's meaningless.

Effectiveness focuses instead on what you did (got done, completed, finished, created, or resolved), how you did it (character, attitude, and behavior), and how you can do it better (efficiency and consistency)? Effective people are able to measure and increase their *value-added* to their employer; enhance their personal and professional development, and do so quicker and easier than they ever could on their own

So, how can you become more effective, when it's not taught anywhere in academia or your company? Here's the good news! That's where we come in. The beauty of *The Effectiveness Guide* is that you can learn *Tactics, Techniques, and Tools* (or best practices) needed to become more effective and successful regardless of your title, position, function, or level of authority, right from your home.

I know from experience that by learning, using, and training others on the *10 Core Competencies of Effectiveness*, you'll become more effective with each passing day. Without your direct intervention in your career, you're leaving your career to chance. You have too much to lose by not taking a more active role in learning the critical skills needed for successful job performance. I know that doing nothing and waiting for someone else to make you more effective, is the definition of complacency, which will kill your career.

If you're ready to elevate-your-game to the next level and become absolutely essential and irreplaceable to any employer lucky enough to have you on his team, *The Effectiveness Guide* will be the best investment you'll ever make in your career.

Also, if you feel this information could help someone else, please take a few moments to let them know. If it turns out to make a difference in their life, they'll be forever grateful to you – as will I.

Let's make a difference together – one person at a time!

All the best!

Ed

Founder of *TheEffectivenessGuide.com*
Coauthor of *The Effectiveness Guide*
email: ed.murphy77@gmail.com

Note: Marked in *Segoe Print* throughout this book, you'll find *Takeaways* or *Key Points* which summarize the main message we wish to convey.

CHAPTER 1:
BY UNDERSTANDING FOLLOWERSHIP

"If I had to reduce the responsibilities of a good follower to a single rule, it would be to speak truth to power."
- Warren Bennis

Leadership and Followership have always been inextricably linked because one cannot be effective or successful without the other.

You cannot be a leader without simultaneously being a follower of someone.

We are all followers of someone. So, don't get upset by being called a *"Follower."* We all have a leader. Even the President of the US has a leader: *The American People.* Even the self-employed, independent contractors, consultants, and entrepreneurs have a leader; whoever pays them for their products or services. The only important question is how do you treat your leader? Do you always do what your leader "likes" and avoid doing what he "dislikes"? If not, you'll hear about it. Do you have good communications with your leader? If not, why? If in doubt, ask!

Effective people know that the influence needed to consistently produce excellent results can only be achieved through the proper and timely application of all *10 Core Competencies of Effectiveness.* The history of America is replete with examples of people who were *wise* enough, *smart* enough, and *driven* enough to realize their shortcomings and to seek out and hire *the best and the brightest* followers they could find to help them became more effective, successful, and rich.

Followership is your ability to support your employer in the accomplishment of his goals.

Most people are quite happy either being the #2 or #3 person in an organization or quietly serving as a member of a staff. However, to be a more effective follower, it helps to understand the roles, stresses, and responsibilities of your leader.

Many times, you will need to be thinking one or two steps ahead of your leader; to anticipate, to see around corners, to smell out mistakes before they become problems, and to see problems before they become a crisis. That's what gives followers their value; their credibility.

This is why behind every effective leader, you'll find a team of dedicated, loyal, and committed followers that ultimately determine their effectiveness and success.

Over the past five decades, serving in the US Military (as a US Army Officer) and in Corporate America (as an Executive Coach), I've been privileged to work with some of America's most exceptional men and women that were real game-changers, self-starters, and effective leaders and followers.

To become absolutely essential to any organization, you must be perceived as someone who can be counted on to consistently produce excellent results and serve the team.

They all had one thing in common. They were able to influence the actions of others by skillfully using the *10 Core Competencies of Effectiveness* (Followership, Delegating, Planning, Organizing, Communicating, Problem-Solving/Decision-Making, Awareness, Training, Motivation, and Character).

CHAPTER 2:
BY KNOWING YOUR "REDCAPS" COLD!

"Followership, like leadership, is a role and not a destination."
- Michael McKinney

To become a more effective tomorrow than you are today, you must know your REDCAPS.

REDCAPS are your responsibilities, expectations, duties, constraints, authority, projects, and standards.

Have you ever been surprised by implied, expected or otherwise fuzzy requirements from your leader? To avoid this, work hard to get clear answers to these questions:

What are your Responsibilities?

Responsibility is an obligation to satisfactorily perform or complete a task that one must fulfill, which has a consequent penalty for failure, and are normally found in your job description and can also be assigned to you by your leader.

Accepting complete responsibility for what you say and do (and what you fail to do and say) and the consequences is the first step to becoming more effective.

Effective followers understand that only their leader bears the ultimate responsibility for both the final decision and the result. Once the decision is made, followers must set aside their personal opinions and get to work executing their leader's decision-as their decision.

What are your Leader's Expectations?

Expectations come directly from your leader and the company. Ask your leader for his expectations and goals for you and take careful notes. If they're not clear, ask for clarification. If something happens that is not expected, it's a surprise, and leaders don't like surprises. What does your leader expect from you in the first 90 days, year?

Also, know your leader's *REDCAPS* and goals, as well as his Focus and Priorities.

What are your Duties?

Your duties are actions that must be satisfactorily performed by a certain time. Your duties are tasks your leader needs you to perform and are normally found in your job description and can also be assigned to you by your leader.

What's the difference between Duties and Responsibilities?

Duties: Actions that must be completed by someone by a stipulated time.

Responsibilities: The burden that is shouldered by someone (*Chapter 5*).

Note: Duties can be assigned and reassigned - responsibility cannot!

What are your Constraints?

Constraints include *imperatives* and *restrictions:*

- *Imperatives* are things you must do (like meeting the goals for your unit)

- *Restrictions* are things you must not do (like not accepting gifts from vendors), which come from your leader and your organization's policies and procedures and include borders and limits.

  - ✓ *Borders* are official/unofficial lines dividing one area from another telling who is responsible for what.

  - ✓ *Limits* are the point at which something ends or beyond which something starts (like the limit of your authority to decide or to act, and when your leader must decide or act).

What Authority do you have?

Authority is your leader's permission given to you to take certain agreed-upon actions on your leader's behalf in support of your official duties and responsibilities.

Authority, unlike responsibility, can be given (granted, limited) to perform a specific assignment. When a leader asks a follower to perform an assignment, he is giving his authority (with limitations stated up-front) to act on his behalf. Authority can include things like the ability to make work assignments, hire and fire, make decisions, or spend money.

What are your Projects?

- *Past* projects that were completed before your arrival
- *Current* projects that are incomplete, pending or remain unfulfilled
- *Future* projects that are coming up soon

What are the Standards?

Standards are the established norm or required minimum level of conformity to organizational policy, criteria, methods, processes, practices, and expectations for both results and behavior. The standard must also satisfy the needs and expectations of your leader and your customer. To find the standards that apply to you, review all organizational guidance, policies, standards of conduct and behavior along with any Standard Operating Procedures (SOP), and your leader's goals.

To put this all together, start by document all your REDCAPS by:

- Carefully reviewing your job description
- Asking your leader for his REDCAPS and goals
- Asking your leader for his expectations of you
- Asking your team members and peers for any hidden REDCAPS
- Asking your predecessor (if available) about any hidden or unstated REDCAPS

CHAPTER 3:
WHAT'S MOST IMPORTANT TO YOUR EMPLOYER?

"Being open to correction means making ourselves vulnerable, and many people are not willing to do that."
- Myles Munroe

Have you ever wondered what's most important and what's not; especially when there are too many things to do and too few hours in the day to get it all done? To survive requires focus and prioritization.

Many new leaders let their leader decide what's most important because they fear making a mistake. However, small business owners, entrepreneurs, and consultants don't have this luxury.

Here, we'll be examining both *Private-Sector Corporations* like Microsoft and *Public-Sector Organizations* like School Districts and Government Agencies, to better understand what's most important to their survival.

What matters most to the survival of
PRIVATE-SECTOR CORPORATIONS?

To help you better understand Focus and Priority, we'll first be examining *Private-Sector Corporations* (like Microsoft) to find out what matters most to their survival. As an Executive Coach, I often asked senior executives from *Private-Sector Companies*, "What matters most to the survival of your company?" The first answer I normally got was People. People are an important resource, but not the most important resource. Just quit your job and see how quickly you'll be replaced. Some said, Technology, which is important, but again, not the most important. So, what really matters most? The only people who don't struggle with this question are Small Business Owners. These guys get it.

Any small business owner will tell you that the most important thing to their survival is Positive Cash Flow.

Without *Positive Cash Flow* (or PCF, the company can't pay their bills, and they're soon out-of-business. Without PCF, the company's bankrupt. Game over! And, according to the *Small Business Administration*, this is the primary reason 80% of start-up companies fail within their first three years.

What about your business unit? If you can link what you and your business unit do for your company's PCF and how it has improved or achieved better results, your business unit is essential to your company. In the same vein, if your business unit can't be directly linked to one or more of the activities that generate PCF, your unit could be considered non-essential and therefore expendable - not a place you want to stay for long. So, what activities generate *Positive Cash Flow*?

Here are the four most important activities that generate *Positive Cash Flow* for *Private-Sector Companies* like Microsoft:

- **Increase Revenues:** To increase revenues from the sale of products and services involves those in sales, marketing, sales support, business development, or strategic development. Can you find and recommend new and innovative ways to sell more products or services like bringing in new customers, selling more to the same customers, discovering new uses for old products, or finding new ways to bring more money in the door, are how revenues are increased.

- **Decrease Operating Costs:** Decreasing operating costs, or saving money, is everyone's job. Can you find and recommend new and innovative ways to reduce costs like consolidating, eliminating, cost sharing, getting a better price from a supplier, conserving, saving time or being more effective, efficient, and consistent?

- **Better Use of Available Resources:** Everyone's job is to better use the resources they already have. Can you find and recommend new and innovative ways to better use the resources your company already has like streamlining, eliminating redundancies, consolidating, conserving, waste reduction, process improvement, reducing time required, becoming more efficient, doing more with less, better maintaining equipment and vehicles to extend their service life, and finding quicker or easier ways of doing things. And how much money or time could be saved annually?

- **Anticipate Problems Today to Save Money Tomorrow:**
  Anticipating problems today to save money tomorrow is also everyone's job. Since lawsuits are very expensive, can you find and recommend new and innovative ways to anticipate problems today to save money tomorrow like creating important policies and procedures, creating better contracts, ensuring the right insurance is in force, ensuring compliance with outside agencies, creating better physical and cybersecurity procedures, creating better property accountability procedures, or eliminating unsafe conditions?

If you work for a *Private-Sector Company* like Microsoft, your career depends on your ability to identify, measure, and increase your *value-added* (individual productivity and sustainability) to one or more of the four activities that contribute to PCF. This step only pertains to half the Job Market. What about all those who are not profit driven like nurses, teachers, firefighter, and all those who put themselves in harm's way every day to defend us and keep us safe? Not every organization is profit driven. So, how do they identify, measure, and increase their value-add?

What matters most to the survival of
PUBLIC-SECTOR ORGANIZATIONS?

Since these organizations do not focus on profit generation, what matters most to them is providing a service that serves the greater good (like schools and government agencies). *Public-Sector Organizations* use what is called a *Band Of Excellence* (BOE) to measure and assess their level of services. For those who work in the *Public-Sector*, like teachers or government workers, they are required to achieve, maintain, or exceed the *Band Of Excellence* (BOE) set by their organization.

So, what is a Band Of Excellence?

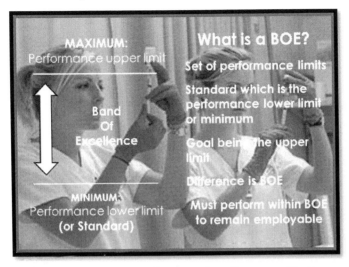

A *Band Of Excellence* (BOE) is a set of performance limits ranging from the Minimum (The Standard) - being the performance lower-limit and the Maximum - being the performance upper-limit.

And the difference between the Minimum and the Maximum is called the *Band of Excellence*. If your performance stays within the *Band of Excellence*, you remain employable.

Here's a simple example:

The biggest government agency on the planet is the *US Department of Defense*. In 1992, as a former US Army Officer, one BOE all soldiers had to meet was the Annual Physical Fitness Test. The BOE Minimum (or Standard) was 200 points overall. The BOE Maximum was 300 points overall. So, the BOE was 200 - 300 for the test overall to remain promotable.

If a Soldier failed to achieve 200 points overall, he was retrained and re-tested. If he failed a second time, he was considered non-promotable and administratively processed for release from the military.

Take teachers and government workers as an example. To remain employable, they're continuously assessed by their supervisors using assessment standards for specific job tasks and behaviors. Employers use these activities to assess both individual and unit performance against their BOEs.

Public-Sector BOEs are measured by daily observations, customer feedback, certification, performance reviews, external audits, visits, compliance inspections, annual qualification, and continuing education. BOE's are used to measure and assess both individual and unit performance, which includes results, behavior, and potential.

As long as each member continues to meet their BOE Standards, they remain employable. If not, they are retrained, retested and either put on probation, reinstated, or released. And, if they achieved or maintained their BOE Maximums, they should expect some form of recognition.

BOE's are needed to measure excellence in *Public-Sector Organizations* because they're not driven by *Positive Cash Flow*. They are used to make periodic assessments to determine if individuals, units, and systems have achieved, maintained or exceeded their BOEs. Without a BOE, you can't measure performance or even tell if you're improving or getting worse.

BOEs are also used by Private-Sector Corporations to help generate Positive Cash Flow.

To create any *Public-Sector Organization*, it must go through these three phases:

Phase 1: Must serve the greater good (schools or government agencies)

Phase 2: Must create a BOE to maintain or enhance that service

Phase 3: Must consistently achieve, maintain, or exceed their BOE for service

This is how they maintain the funding needed to operate, which comes from city, state, and federal tax revenues. And, if the organization can no longer meet their BOE Standards for services, they run the risk of losing their funding.

If you work for a *Public-Sector Organization*, like school districts or government agencies, your career depends on your ability to identify, measure, and increase your BOE *value-added*.

Summary: The two things every company in the world must have to survive:

- *Private-Sector Companies* (like Microsoft) must generate PCF and achieve, maintain, or exceed their BOEs

- *Public-Sector Organizations* (like School Districts) must achieve, maintain, or exceed their BOEs to receive funding

CHAPTER 4:
BY "ADDING-VALUE" TO YOUR EMPLOYER

"Do what you can, with what you have, where you are."
- Theodore Roosevelt

Here's a true story:

One day, Bob was called for a job interview for a job that he really wanted. This new job came with a promotion and doubled his salary. You know the drill; this is where you get the chance to justify your existence to complete strangers. As expected, Bob was nervous, especially when the interviewer started out by asking him, "Why should we hire you?"

After Bob picked himself up off the floor, he stammered something that most people would say, "Well, I was responsible for...." Then, to make things worse, the interviewer actually interrupted him and said, "Stop! No one cares what you were responsible for. I want to know what you achieved. What got better because you were there? What was your value-added (individual productivity and sustainability) to your leader?"

Unfortunately, Bob didn't get the job, which was a shame because he was the best of all of those they interviewed. He just didn't know his *value-added*. Bob didn't know how to sell himself. This story, unfortunately, is the norm rather than the exception. All too often good people have no clue what's most important to a potential employer or how to articulate their *value-added*. Has this ever happened to you? If not, it will. But, by reading this guide, you'll never hesitate to answer these questions.

Your *value-added* is quite simply tour effectiveness; the sum of everything you bring to the table (like your knowledge, skills, experience, achievements, attitude, relationships, character, and balance) that has contributed, in some measurable and significant way, to the achievement of your leader's goals.

You already know how important it is to your career to be able to add value to your leader. But, did you know that most people have no clue how to do that? The problem comes from the fact that few people truly understand what matters most to the survival of their organization.

Once you learn how to identify, measure, and increase your value-added to your leader, you're well on the way to becoming absolutely essential to any employer.

Most people only begin to identify their *value-added* near the end of their career, if at all. To identify your *value-added* (individual productivity and sustainability), here are the most important questions to ask to determine how you're linked to PCF/BOE.

To help you determine how you (and your business unit) are linked to the things that matter most, you need answers to these questions: Do you know your leader's goals? If not, ask; Are your leader's goals measurable? Do your goals contribute directly to your leader's goals? Are your goals measurable?

If not, continue to collaborate with your leader until you can answer Yes to the above questions.

Are your duties essential to the survival of your company?

How do you help others and who are you helping? Most members don't deal directly with customers. Most often, your #1 customer will be another member or unit of your company.

What's the Band of Excellence?

How do you contribute to your leader's PCF/BOE Goals? Standards here mean the minimum acceptable level of performance (results and behavior). This includes the stated, inherent, and expected standards for the duties you perform. Where's the line between the acceptable and unacceptable? What does your leader expect of your performance (results and behavior)?

How does your leader measure your performance?

Who does the measuring? What are the metrics and how often does your leader make assessments? How does your performance compare to your peers? Compare to your peers means those at your same level as teachers in the same school. Although not the best method for comparison, it's important to collaborate with your peers because you'll learn a lot.

The best way to measure your performance is to compare yourself to where you were a year ago.

Are you getting better or staying the same?

Staying the same is the same as getting worst. How do you know for sure? Who is counting or measuring? What are the metrics? Are you getting better over time? If so, how much better? Without measuring and keeping track of how you're doing, how can you ever answer this question?

What do you get for being the best or for improving? Are there incentives in place for continuously excellent performance? Have you received awards, promotions, raises, accolades, kudos, or other recognition? Do you have copies of this recognition? What was the recognition for? What did you do to earn it?

If you're not improving over time, guess what your peers are doing?

This also includes professional development, which means additional education, training, and certifications. From the first day you started, until today, what have you done or recommended to be done that got better because you were there? What was your contribution to moving the work forward? What have you done to make your performance more effective, efficient, and consistent?

Answering these questions will help you determine how you (and your unit) are linked to the things that matter most: your leader's PCF/BOE goals.

CHAPTER 5:
BY BEING "ACCOUNTABLE" TO YOUR EMPLOYER

"Followers are more important to leaders than leaders are to followers."
- Barbara Kellerman

You are accountable to your leader for everything that happens or fails to happen within your areas of responsibility. Accountability is the acknowledgment and assumption of responsibility for actions, products, decisions, and policies including the administration, governance, and implementation within the scope of the role or employment position and encompassing the obligation to report, explain, and be answerable for resulting consequences.

Accountability cannot exist unless you know all the things (people, processes, goals, facilities, and equipment) for which you are responsible, which is normally found in your Job Description.

Accountability is often confused with responsibility and is normally not a problem until something goes wrong.

For example, if something goes wrong within your area of responsibility, you will get the chance to explain to your leader, and his leader, what happened and what is being done to ensure it never happens again. Sometimes, depending on the severity of the problem, your leader will not be happy with you.

What most people don't understand is that *Responsibility* and *Accountability* go together; they're part of the same *iceberg*.

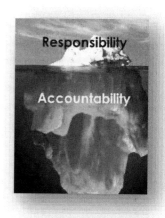

Unfortunately, you can't see the *Accountability* part of the *iceberg* because it lies hidden beneath the surface until something goes wrong. When things go wrong, which they will, your leader's job is to ask you for an explanation.

What your leader doesn't need is for you to play the blame game, make excuses, or hide the truth.

Instead take these actions; First, Investigate - what happened and what caused it to happen? Second, *Return and Report* - report to your leader the facts and your recommendation. Third, Fix it & Fix it for good! And, finally, *Return and Report* - when fixed, report the fix to your leader.

Establish the reputation of being a good problem solver as well as a good problem finder. Leader's like it when you anticipate problems before they become a crisis. Your job is to help your leader find, fix, and eliminate all distractions or obstacles that could slow or stop the achievement of his goals.

When things go wrong, don't take it personally, take it professionally and fix it.

We all make mistakes. This is how we learn. However, mistakes, errors, and defects are not a problem if they're caught and fixed before they leave your unit. The *acid-test* for accountability is the absence of blaming others and making excuses. What systems (checks, procedures, rehearsals, *preventive actions*, QC, or Testing) are in place to catch mistakes and errors before they leave your unit?

What is Personal Accountability?

Personal accountability is not something you're born with. It comes as you mature and become a *Fully Functioning Adult*. Unfortunately, very few of those you'll meet in the workplace have a fully developed sense of *personal accountability or maturity*. This is your chance to stand out above the rest.

Personal accountability is a willingness to accept the consequences of your actions/inactions; what you say and do, what you fail to say and do, and how it affects those around you.

It's also an obligation and duty to ensure your good character and behavior regardless of how you were brought up or what kind of conditioning you've received.

When you fully accept that you're completely accountability for yourself, and realize that no one is coming to your rescue, this is the beginning of peak performance.

And, there's very little you can't do or have after you accept this motto:

"If it is to be, it is up to me!" – Anonymous

Do you do your Best Work every day?

Some people are quite happy doing the minimums just to get by. For others, only their best is good enough. Which are you?

Here's a great story about doing your best work:

*It's rumored that when Dr. **Henry Kissinger** was Secretary of State, in the administrations of Presidents Nixon and Ford, he asked for a security assessment be made of a foreign country.*

The next day, when a subordinate delivered the report, Secretary Kissinger asked, "Is this your best work?" The subordinate thought for a second and walked out of the office.

The next day, the subordinate returned with the report and Kissinger asked the same question. The subordinate again thought for a moment and walked back out of the office.

The following day, the subordinate returned, and Kissinger asked for the third time, "Is this your best work?" This time the subordinate said, "Yes." Kissinger then responded, "Good, now I'll read it."

I share this story to highlight the fact that there are no shortcuts to greatness. Your success will always be linked to *"doing your best work."* Do you do your best work every day? Would your leader agree?

CHAPTER 6:
BY CONTRIBUTING TO
YOUR EMPLOYER'S MEETING

"It is the men behind who make the man ahead."
-Merle Crowell

Your employer 's meetings are important because they may be the only contact or observation your leader has of your performance. It will be attended by your employer's other Direct Reports; your peers.

As such, here are a few things "TO DO" when attending your employer's meetings:

- Arrive 15 minutes early to get to know your peers
- Display dignity, respect, and kindness
- Be more supportive of your employer (*Chapter 15*)
- Do everything you can to support your peers (Teamwork is critical)
- Put your cell phone on vibrate or leave it in your office
- Demonstrate that you're a Team Player by your 100% attention, involvement, and participation
- Come with the attitude to contribute, encourage, and help others
- Understand the two most important things to any employer (*Chapter 3*)

And, here are a few things "NOT TO DO":

- Surprise your employer
- Embarrass a peer
- Find fault or complain

CHAPTER 7:
BY "FOLLOWING UP"
& "FOLLOWING THROUGH"

"Employees do a great deal more following than leading, even as leaders. For the most part, followership behaviors drive tactical successes. Leadership talents and skills propel strategic accomplishments."
-Rodger Adair

One of the biggest problems new leaders experience is a failure to *Follow up* and *Follow through*.

What's *Follow Up?*

Follow up is a subsequent action taken if there is no response (or a negative response) to an initial action.

There are three types of *Follow up*:

Type 1: *What you do when someone declines to buy from you (negative response)*

Using a sales example, if a prospect declines to do business with you, you still have an obligation to following up. If you sent a letter, email, or voicemail and received no reply, *Follow up* means continuing to contact them, until they respond. Continue to add value to your relationship; to help the person you are trying to contact.

Type 2: *What you do when trying to contact someone to correct a problem*

If you are trying to contact someone to resolve a problem (like poor customer service, a faulty product, or a delayed order), record the date you called, whom you spoke with, and the response you received. Always leave a voicemail message giving your name, phone number, a description of the problem, and a request for a return call.

Always document your *Follow up* action. After you've called several times, sent several letters, with no response, show up and get your problem resolved.

Type 3: What you do when you ask someone, who does not report to you, to do something (commonly called checking)

The third type of *Follow up* comes when you ask someone not a Direct Report (like your leader, peer, vendor, supplier, or friend) to do something. *Follow up* by contacting them a few days before the deadline to ensure everything gets done.

For example, let's assume you're responsible for organizing a company luncheon for your employer. As you review your *Assignments Tracking Sheet*, a few days before the luncheon, here's what you might say on the phone to a vendor:

> *"Hi, Mary. This is Joe from ABC Company. I'm calling (no email reminders) to confirm the luncheon for Tuesday, October 10th, at 11:30 AM? (Exactly what you asked her to do a month ago. Be specific!).*
>
> *Is everything still on track? Any problems or concerns? Did you get the change to the headcount? We're now expecting 50 people, not 25. Okay - Great!*
>
> *I know you'll do a great job! (Encouragement!)*
>
> *Please call me if there are any changes, questions, or problems. Here's my cell number, 816.xxx.xxxx. Thanks again Mary and I look forward to seeing you on Tuesday."*

Also, during the luncheon, ensure someone (hopefully, you) publicly thanks Mary and her whole team for a wonderful luncheon – that's real character!

What's *Follow Through*?

Follow through is the process of returning to the asker, either face-to-face or on the phone, and reporting the status of their request.

There are two types of *Follow through*:

Type 1: *What you do after your leader or customer asks you to do something.*

Make sure you have a clear understanding of what they want done (the end-result) and when they need it completed (the Deadline). If you have questions, ask! If you can't deliver, speak up!

Then, *Follow through* (*Return and Report* via face-to-face or phone) after completing the assignment. If you cannot complete the assignment as requested, *Follow through* (*Return and Report),* explain the problem, and what you recommend be done to resolve it.

Always under-promise and over-deliver!

Without *Follow through*, your leader or customer has no idea what's happening. Let them know what you're doing. Be responsive – *Follow through* as soon as possible. If you *Follow through*, you'll stand out from the rest.

Return and Report is the most important part of Follow through!

Type 2: *What you do after asking a Direct Report to do something.*

When you ask a Direct Report to do something, ensure you tell them WHAT you want done (the end-result) and WHEN you need it completed (the deadline). Ask them to *Follow through* (*Return and Report,* via face-to-face or call) when completed.

Avoid telling them HOW to do it-unless they're clueless.

Also, if they cannot complete the assignment, ask them to *Follow through* (*Return and Report),* explain the problem, and what they recommend be done to resolve it.

In fact, the best people I know do something special, they Over-Communicate! They Follow through even if they have nothing new to report. This way, I knew I wasn't forgotten!

CHAPTER 8:
BY BEING "PROACTIVE"

"The world is moved not only by the mighty shoves of heroes, but also by the aggregate of the tiny pushes of each honest worker."
- Helen Keller

Another way to become more effective is by being proactive.

A proactive person is someone who identifies and prevents potential problems.

A proactive person is someone who creates or controls a situation by causing something to happen rather than responding after it happens. Being proactive requires that you:

- Anticipating your leader's needs, F*ollow up* and *Follow through (Chapter 7),* as needed

- Identify potential mistakes before they become a problem and problems before they become a crisis

- Do NOT wait to be told exactly what to do. If you don't know, find out!

- *Take charge* of your assigned duties and responsibilities and make things happen the right way the first time

- Be enterprising, energetic, driven, bold, and *take-charge*

Being proactive also means that you are proficient in how to take *Immediate Action (Appendix B).*

How Self-Correcting are you?

Part of being proactive is being self-correcting especially when starting a new position, even if it's within the same organization. Starting anything new is all about learning what must be learned, as soon as possible. I'm constantly amazed by all those who never take notes. Why is that? Why do so few people take notes anymore?

"A short pencil is a long memory." - *Unknown*

When you have a question, write it down; don't trust your memory. Many times, the person with the correct answer won't be immediately available. If you find a term you don't understand, write it down.

Later, find out what the term means. Keep a list of all your questions and the terms you don't understand. This will help later when you get the chance to sponsor a new member into your team.

Those who are *self-correcting*, take notes-they don't trust their memory, write down their questions and the answers, are unafraid to ask questions, and proactively seek out answers to their questions.

- When you make a mistake, have the moral courage to admit it, fix it, and learn from it.

- When you hurt someone's feelings, or your behavior was inappropriate, have the moral courage to apologize, say you're sorry, make no excuses, and don't do it again.

Why no excuses? Making excuses diminishes your sincerity and makes you sound like you're trying to hide behind your excuse. You're human, and humans make mistakes. Most importantly, there's no excuse for bad behavior.

TRAINING: To learn more about awareness and being *Self-Correcting*, review the movie, *Ground Hog Day*, with **Bill Murray.** Then conduct a group discussion answering these questions: How is your life similar to the movie? How is your life different from the movie? How can you use what you've learned here to become more effective?

CHAPTER 9:

BY GIVING "SITUATION REPORTS"

"From Gandhi to Mandela, from the American patriot to the Polish shipbuilders, the makers of revolutions have not come from the top."
- Gary Hamel

What do you say when your leader stops by, or calls you on the phone, and asks, *"What's up?, What's happening, or How's it going"?* Your leader is asking you for a *Situation Report.*

If you want to stand out from your peers, give your leader a 30 second, *Situation Report.* Try this!

When asked about your status, give your leader the answer to these questions:

- What are you currently working on?

- When do you expect to finish?

- What are your *Changes* and *Unresolved Issues? (Appendix F).*

Here's an example of a *Situation Report*:

One day, Bob took the entire day to visit all his Direct Reports at their office and asked, "What's goin on?" Most said things like, "Not much, we're okay, or same ole same-o."

However, one Direct Report said, "We're working on Project Alpha which should be done by Friday. We had to change the format slightly because we couldn't get the Executive Summary to fit on one page. By the way, we still need the input from Accounting. Can you help with that?"

Bob was impressed and said, "Nice work! Thanks. I'll look into that input you need from Accounting."

The first time you give a *Situation Report*, your leader will be stunned, and you'll gain instant credibility. Also, whenever you identify a problem, bring it to your leader with your recommendation of several reasonable solutions.

CHAPTER 10:
BY ACCEPTING NEW ASSIGNMENTS

*"It takes half your life before you discover
life is a do-it-yourself project."*
- Napoleon Hill

In the workplace, if you *"accept an assignment,"* this starts the Planning Phase of the Project Process. This means you have been asked by your leader to do something (task or project) and you accepted. If you accepted, you've promised to deliver, but will you?

Do you have to accept every
Assignment from your Employer?

Actually, *No*. You have five things you can do. If you *accept* the project or don't say anything, you just made a promise to deliver. A promise also includes when you tell someone you'll do something or when you're asked for help, and you say you'll help. If you're not going to help, then say so!

Keep your word, especially to yourself,
or don't make the promise in the first place.

Whether you promise a friend, associate, your leader, a total stranger, or yourself that you'll do something by a certain time, you've already created a debt. And, if you're poor at keeping your promises, this will destroy your credibility.

The toxic effect of this debt is catastrophic to your relationships, as well as your self-image. If it's a bad habit, own up to it and make the change. Do you deliver on what you said you'd do? If you tell someone, *"I'll get back to you,"* do you?

Your greatest personal power is your word.
Under promise and over deliver!

The person doing the asking could be a superior (your leader in most cases), or it could be a peer or even a subordinate.

However, just because someone asks you to do something doesn't mean you must accept.

Here are the five Options you have when asked to do anything:

- **If you Accept**, you begin the process of receiving the project. Accepting a project means you've been selected by someone (normally your leader) to be *in-charge* of making something (the project) happen and you agreed to accept.

  Do not accept if you cannot deliver. Stop and think. If you have any concerns or reservations, say so. When you first receive a project, it's important you identify two things: what needs to be done and the deadline?

  Be careful not to accept too much, which will burn you out. Accepting too much and being afraid or too proud to say NO or ask for help, is a recipe for disaster. If you intend to remain effective over the long haul, ensure you know your workload.

  Part of being effective is knowing when to say NO and when to ask for help.

- **If you Accept with Conditions**, state your reasons and negotiate the conditions. Negotiating is the most underrated skill a person can have and one of the most productive. When you consider that most human communication is some form of negotiating, you'll quickly come to realize how important this skill is to your ability to influence others. Can you say NO to your leader? Of course, just make sure you have a good reason. Now the negotiations begin.

- **If you Delay**, by telling someone that you'll get back with them, do you? Remember, your integrity and credibility are being tested here. Keep your word.

- **If you Redirect**, ensure you direct them to someone (or somewhere) that can help them. Helping others builds relationships. If you can't help them or they can help themselves, direct them to the solution. Be helpful.

- **If you Reject,** ensure you have a good reason. Can you reject your leader? Sure, but he'll need a good reason. Also, be prepared to negotiate because your leader may have no other choice. Be assertive and tell your leader specifically what you need, along with the consequences and effects of what won't get done.

CHAPTER 11:

BY NEGOTIATING NEW ASSIGNMENTS

"You do not get what you want. You get what you negotiate."
- Harvey Mackay

Before you accept any project, make sure you negotiate the details. Do you have the time and other resources needed to accomplish the project? What is the requirement and scope (complexity) of the project? Here are some other things you should consider.

Put yourself in the position of your Leader:

What objections do you expect? What response do you have to these objections? Many people are afraid or too proud to negotiate and/or ask for help. Just by asking for something, you have a 66% chance of getting something. Every time you ask for something, your leader can either say, *YES, NO,* or he can, *split the difference.* The better you negotiate, the more you'll receive.

Know the difference between a Need and a Want:

What you *need*, is more important than what you *want*. Be more assertive. Tell your leader, *"I need ... "*, and then justify it.

The stronger your justification - the higher your Probability of Success.

And, if you get turned down, bring out all the negative effects (consequences) that could occur.

Increase your Leverage and Justification:

Leverage is the power you have when your leader really needs you to do something quickly.

The more your leader wants something done, the more *leverage* you have. The more *leverage* you have, the greater the probability your request will be granted. Accepting a project is a negotiation.

Your leader wants to get going on the project. If you need something, the time to ask is before you accept the project. If you wait and ask later, your *leverage* is gone. The only power you have left is *justification.*

Justification is the <u>compelling reason</u> you're asking.

The most important things you can do to increase your justification are:

- Link your request to helping the Organization or Unit.

Example: "I need this new technology because it will dramatically increase the quality of what we produce."

- Link your request to achieving, maintaining, or exceeding your goals

- Link your request to one of your leader's priorities

- Link your request to effectiveness, efficiency, or consistency

- Show how granting your request will make your leader look good

- Compare yourself to someone who's already received it. (*You said YES to Joe last week*)

- Explain how your request is making up for something you were previously denied

- You deserve it because you've done a great job in the past or appeal to your leader's sense of fairness

Be prepared to justify your request and prepare a persuasive argument to address any objections presented by your leader. If turned down, be ready to present the adverse consequences.

Ask for MORE than you need:

When you ask for anything, your leader can answer three different ways. He can say, *Yes.* He can say, *No.* And, he can *split the difference* and give you half of what you asked for. Anticipate this. If you're negotiating budget money for a project and you want $5,000, ask for $10,000 instead. This way your leader can think he's winning the negotiation by granting you $5,000.

CHAPTER 12:
BY AVOIDING THE
"CAUSES" OF PROJECT FAILURE

***"It's fine to celebrate success but it is more important
to heed the lessons of failure."***
– Bill Gates

Did you ever have an assignment that had problems; things that did not seem to go as you expected?

The potential causes of project failure are:

- Assumed the resources needed would be available

- Forgot!!! (*Appendix G*)

- Assumed others would show up to help, and no one showed

- Failed to delegate (tried to do everything yourself)

- Failed to elevate problems to his leader and didn't fully understand the project Objective

- Made invalid and/or *unconscious assumptions (Appendix A)*

- Failed to use any *Preventive Actions (Appendix C)*

- Failed to track changes and *Unresolved Issues (Appendix F)*.

- *Abdicated,* failed to *Follow through* (Check & *Return & Report*) *(Chapter 7)*

- Failed to give *Progress Briefing* to his leader *(Appendix A)*

- Waited until the last-minute to resolve problems

- Failed to *Take Charge (Appendix B)*

- Failed to track Assignments *Accepted* and *Assigned (Appendix A)*

- Failed to give a *Backbriefing* to his leader *(Appendix D)*

- Failed to demonstrate good judgment

How do you demonstrate Good Judgment?

"Experience is simply the name we give our mistakes."
- Oscar Wilde

Good decisions don't happen by accident.

- Good decisions come from good judgment
- Good judgment comes from failure
- Failure comes from mistakes
- Mistakes come from bad decisions
- Bad decisions come from bad judgment
- Bad judgment comes from a lack of experience or impairment (fatigue, negative emotions, drugs, distractions, etc.)
- Lack of experience comes from:
  - ✓ Having little time invested on the job
  - ✓ Not learning from your mistakes (lack of common-sense, competence, or commitment)
  - ✓ Not learning from the mistakes of others

Learning from the mistakes of others only happens if you're paying attention. Paying attention and learning from the mistakes of others is what this guide is all about. The truth is that anyone can cut their learning curve and gain years of valuable experience by understanding and using this simple principle:

We all make mistakes. That's how we learn.
You can also learn from the mistakes of others,
but only if you're paying attention.

Remember, there's a big difference between the decision and the result of the decision. You could be the most talented and experienced decision-maker on the planet, and you could make the best decision, but there's no guarantee that the result will be positive or even resolve the problem.

You can make a good decision, and the results could still be a disaster because the situation, facts, and assumptions that were available when you first made the decision could (and will) change over time. What was good today could turn out to be bad tomorrow.

In the end, only you can define success and failure for your life. Everything you do, or fail to do, has consequences, sometimes good, sometimes – not so much.

TRAINING: To learn more about good judgment and risk-taking, review the *Hallmark* movie, *New in Town*, with **Renée Zellweger** and **Harry Connick Jr.,** a comedy about how a small town in Minnesota. Then, conduct a group discussion answering these questions: What examples of both good and bad judgment did you find in the movie? What kinds of risks did *Zellweger* take to make things happen? How can you use what you've learned here to become more effective?

CHAPTER 13:
BY CONDUCTING PROJECTS

"Coming together is a beginning; keeping together is progress; working together is success."
- Henry Ford

Before you accept an assignment, ask all your questions upfront to ensure you understand your REDCAPS (Responsibilities, Expectations, Duties, Constraints, Authority, Projects, and Standards), which must be identified to avoid any hidden surprises. Also, ensure you have a clear understanding of the purpose of the assignment, why it's important, the Objective (or desired end-state), how it will be measured and by whom, and your access to relevant information.

Your most important duties AFTER accepting a New Project are:

- Provide a *Backbriefing* to your leader using our POA format, so nothing is left out *(Appendix D)*.

- Provide your leader periodic *Progress Briefing* to ensure he knows what's going on *(Appendix A)*

- Defer major decisions to your leader with recommended solutions

- Ask your Delegatees if they're prepared and have no changes or *Unresolved Issues (Appendix F)*.

- Ask your Delegatees to *Follow through* and *Return and Report* to you *(Chapter 7)*

- Ask for more than you need (10% won't get the word or won't be able to deliver)

- Ask that the required people and equipment arrive before you really need them

- Carefully *Track* all your tasks/projects both *accepted* and *made*, changes, and *Unresolved Issues (Appendix F)*.

- Retain your *Flexibility to Respond* to unforeseen circumstances *(Appendix A)*

- Have *Contingency Plans* ready for anticipated problems *(Appendix E)*.

- Stay connected, know what's going on, and be prepared to take *Immediate Action (Appendix B)*.

- *Follow through* with your leader and your Delegatees (*Chapter 7*) repeat above

If you ever feel you can't accomplish the objective, tell your leader immediately. He will need to provide additional resources to arrive at a *workable* solution.

CHAPTER 14:
BY GIVING AND RECEIVING "FEEDBACK"

"Feedback is the Breakfast of Champions"
- Ken Blanchard

How do you give Feedback to your Team Members?

Have you ever worked for someone who seldom/never gave you feedback as to how you were doing? How did that make you feel? If you're looking to improve your performance or the performance of your unit, feedback helps to make the adjustments and corrections needed.

The goal of feedback is to identify the gap between desired and actual performance (for results and behavior, of individuals, teams, units, and systems), and to close the gap ASAP. If you don't receive feedback, ask for it; not only from your leader but from others.

Feedback can occur anytime but normally comes during audits, performance-oriented training, performance appraisals and reviews, shareholders' meeting, marketing research, 360-degree feedback, peak performance coaching, visits and observations, on-site inspections, surveys, meetings, and *After-Action Reviews.*

The most important steps of the Feedback Loop for Human Performance are:

Step 1, Evidence: The performance must be measured, recorded, and assessed.

Step 2, Relevance: Feedback must be relayed to the member in a context that makes sense.

Step 3, Consequence: Feedback must clearly illuminate a path to improvement.

Step 4, Action: Member must decide to change their actual performance to come closer to the desired performance.

Then, that new performance can be re-measured, and the feedback loop can run once more, every action stimulating new performance that moves the member closer to the desired performance.

If you fail to provide periodic and specific feedback to your members, your silence will speak louder than words. It's your job to let them know how they're doing.

If corrective action is appropriate (like someone failed to meet a specific standard), do so in private. Take a moment to ensure the member knew the correct standard and didn't have a good reason for doing (or failing to do) what he did.

Sometimes positive and negative feedback is confused with *praise* and *criticism*. In contrast to feedback, telling someone your opinion does not constitute as feedback unless they act on your suggestion, and thus cause you to revise your opinion.

How do you receive Feedback?

When you reccive feedback, you get to decide how you'll apply it, how you'll react or respond, and if you'll use it to become more effective, efficient, and consistent.

Feedback is often perceived as a euphemism for criticism, as in "My Boss gave me feedback on...." Don't let this happen to you. If you just "blow it off," you'll never get any better. You don't have to agree. In fact, initially, you won't. However, arguing or being defensive sends the wrong message.

You need the feedback, no matter how painful, embarrassing, or ridiculous, because without it, you'll be the same next year as you are today. Also, the person giving the feedback, in many cases, could have a say in your future. Be self-correcting! Prove that you are listening and getting better every day.

Effective people thrive on feedback because their goal is to be "self-correcting."

When you receive feedback from anyone, respond with gratitude and thank them for their honesty.

If you don't receive feedback, ask for it. It will make you more effective!

CHAPTER 15:
BY GIVING "FEEDBACK" TO YOUR EMPLOYER

"We all need people who will give us feedback.
That's how we improve."
- Bill Gates

Should you provide feedback to your employer? Absolutely! In fact, you owe it to your leader. This is called ~~moral courage~~ and is the toughest part of being loyal to your employer; telling him what he doesn't want to hear - like the truth.

It's your job to keep your employer informed. You do that by getting your employer's approval to be honest and make sure you're somewhere private.

Privately providing honest feedback to your employer
is the stronger half of courage and loyalty.

You might suggest that you both take a walk to somewhere private where you won't be interrupted or overheard. Start by saying, *"I need to give you some feedback on..."* or *"I just wanted to tell you how I feel about...."* or *"I just thought you needed to know."* When was the last time you took your employer for a walk and discussed what's really going on?

There is a *fine-line* between *tattling* on someone and reporting the facts. When you report something as being unsafe, you are doing it to stop someone from getting hurt.

The goal of reporting is to keep someone out of trouble (which includes your employer). When people *tattle,* it's about getting someone else in trouble. Just report the facts without embellishing.

Do you have good communication with your employer? If not, why? If in doubt, ask!

CHAPTER 16:
BY ENHANCING YOUR "CREDIBILITY"

"I want someone where I have confidence and credibility that they're up to the job and that I can trust what they tell me."
- Karl Rove

Do followers need credibility? You bet! In fact, without credibility (believability), a follower cannot become effective. For any employer to have faith in a follower, the issues always involve credibility. And, credibility always involves your performance and character.

How does your employer measure your performance? Measuring performance is the process of comparing the difference between the desired and the actual performance and includes measuring two things; your results and behavior.

How does your leader assess your RESULTS?

What are results? Results are what you achieve and include actual job outputs, countable products, measurable outcomes and accomplishments, and the goals you've achieved, maintained or exceeded. However, your results must be something under your control, regardless of whether the result is mental or physical. Your results could be a mental result like answers or recommendations. Your results should be something you can measure and record for your next performance review. Results are normally measured objectively (via numbers or metrics) and don't have to be observed.

Are your results consistent? What happens to unsuccessful NFL Football Coaches near the end of every season? They get fired! It's not Personal; it's Business! If you can't produce the desired result, your employer will be looking for someone who can. He has no choice unless he wants his position to be in question.

Do your results contribute to your employer's goals? If your results consistently contribute to your employer's goals, you're in good shape.

To learn the two most important things every employer in the world must do/have to survive, review *Chapter 3*.

How does your leader assess your BEHAVIOR (or Character)?

Your behavior, on the other hand, includes your competencies, skills, expertise, and proficiencies, your adherence to organizational values, customer feedback, supplier feedback, and your personal style, manners, and approach. Behavior also includes how you treat others (what you say and do, plus what you fail to say and do) and is normally measured subjectively (personal assessment).

Does your behavior reflect positively on the organization's standards and expectations? How do you treat your team members and customers? Do you treat everyone with dignity, respect, and kindness?

These are the things effective employer consider when assessing your behavior. Are you a good example to those around you? Would they agree? Character (your behavior) counts!

In fact, character is the most important considerations when it comes to assessing anyone's future potential. Are you supportive of your employer? How would your employer rate your support? Any room for improvement? (*Chapter 17*)

CHAPTER 17:
BY SUPPORTING YOUR EMPLOYER

"True leadership must have follower-ship.
Management styles can vary, but even an autocrat needs
people who believe and simply don't follow from fear."
— James Robinson III, RRE Ventures

Another way to become more effective is by being more supportive of your employer. How well you support your employer? How do you know for sure? Would your employer agree?

Here's a list of the most important things that employers care about when evaluating their employees. Effective employees take this assessment annually to ensure they remain effective and irreplaceable.

EMPLOYER SUPPORT ASSESSMENT

Using the legend below, assess your answer to these *Support Statements*.

Strongly Agree = 3; Agree = 2; N/A = Non-Applicable;
Disagree = 1; Strongly Disagree = 0

1. I do all I can to help my employer achieve his goals, no matter what!

2. I treat everyone with dignity, respect, and kindness

3. I always do my best work every day

4. I know my REDCAPS and get things done the right way the first time!

5. I'm a Team Player: I cooperate, coordinate, and collaborate.

6. I deal honestly with others - revealing problems and telling the whole story

7. I proactively anticipate problems before they become a crisis

8. I'm *self-correcting* and catch mistakes/errors before my employer /customer

9. I recommend solutions to problems I encounter

10. I play by the rules, unless I have a good reason for not doing so

11. I continuously seek ways to improve what I do

12. I improve my skills through further education and training

13. I achieve, maintain, or exceed my goals

14. I'm accountable for my actions, omissions, and the consequences

15. I do all I can to support the members with whom I work

16. I ensure my employer is the first to hear any bad news

17. When asked or expected to do something, I *Follow through (Chapter 7)*.

18. If I don't know, I ask

19. If I'm supposed to know, but don't, I find out & *Return & Report* ASAP *(Chapter 7)*.

20. I contribute to my employer's meetings, activities, and events

21. I cease discussion when my employer makes the final decision

22. I support my employer's decisions, as my decision, especially if I disagree

23. I give *Situation Reports (Chapter 9)*, with deadlines, *Unresolved Issues (Appendix F)*, and changes

24. I ensure my focus and priorities reinforce my employer 's

25. I do all I can to avoid last-minute surprises to my employer

26. I do all I can to avoid wasting my employer 's time

27. I show a positive attitude

28. I never speak badly of others unless in my employer's office, privately

29. I stay home and call my employer if I have the common signs of being sick

30. When my employer asks me to do something, I do it, and *Return & Report*

All these statements above are things you directly control and can therefore change.

Personal Assessment:

- For all statements you scored a 3: Here you Strongly Agreed. Good!

- For all statements you scored a 2: Here you Agreed. Good, but what needs to be done to score a 3?

- For all statements you scored N/A: Why doesn't this apply to you? Does your employer concur?

- For all statements you scored a 1: Here you Disagreed. Why? What can you do to raise it to a 2?

- For all statements you scored a 0: Why do you Strongly Disagree? Does your employer concur?

Any room for improvement? Your goal should be to consistently achieve a "Strongly Agree" with all the statements above.

If you have doubts, ask!
The only stupid question is the one you're afraid to ask, because later on –when you don't know the answer–you will look stupid.

Additionally, to Best support your employer, you must:

- Know your employer's intent, responsibilities, expectations, projects, goals, and standards

- Know your employer's values, priorities, idiosyncrasies, strengths, and weaknesses

- Have access to information sharing and processing

- Gain permission to voice your honest opinion, behind closed doors, without fear of negative consequences

- Know your employer's expectations of tradition and culture

Note: If you intend to remain effective over the long-term, be sensitive to the things your employer needs to support him and the team.

THE END!

Congratulations! You've reached the end of this book. Thank you for reading! Please remember to share what you've learned here with others. If you help others succeed, they'll return the favor.

This book was about how to enhance your career potential by becoming a more effective tomorrow than you are today. My effective people with whom I had the privilege to work with made it clear how much they valued and trusted us.

They knew that they could never have achieved their level of effectiveness and success without our consistent drive for excellence. They knew the secret; they knew how to treat others with dignity, respect, and kindness. This is why I served them to the best of my ability regardless of their title, position or level of authority.

If you use these small and simple things, in the service of others, you will become absolutely essential to any employer lucky enough to have you on his team.

I've told their story – my job's done. It's now your turn to teach what you've learned through your example of serving others. I have great faith in your potential. You can do this!

Get out of your Comfort Zone and let your struggles drive you to greatness!

I pray that you might have a greater desire to serve the people in your organization, community, church, and family.

If you found this book to be of value, you'll also find value in the other books from *The Effectiveness Guide* series (see Other Books). The subjects covered are designed to help you enhance your career by teaching you how to become absolutely essential to any organization as you become more effective with each passing day.

*You can do this! I have faith in you.
What's holding you back?*

Self-Assessment:

After reading this book:

- How can you use what you've learned to become more effective tomorrow today than you were yesterday?

- How can you use it to become absolutely essential and irreplaceable to any employer?

- How can you use what you've learned outside of work (in your community, church, or family) to become more effective?

- Who else could use it to become more effective?

Do something meaningful with your life. Pay it forward.
Help someone else rise.

ACKNOWLEDGMENTS

*"Many people will walk in and out of your life, but only
true friends will leave footprints in your heart."*
- Eleanor Roosevelt

I'd like to recognize those with whom I've had the pleasure of serving, whose Effectiveness and Character I vividly recall, many of whom are not here today to tell their story.

For my military career, I thank Betty McInte, Edward J. Murphy (my Dad), Dale R. Nelson, Geoffrey "Jeff" Prosch, Craig "Randy" Rutler, Dave Wagner, John Andrews, John "The Bear" Warren, John "Jack" Costello, Dan Labin, and Ron Nicholl for their example of Effectiveness.

*To my fellow Brothers and Sisters-in-Arms, I thank you
for your faithful service to our nation, especially
those who have fallen in the line-of-duty.*

Special thanks to my long-time mentor and friend, Joyce Kuntz, who encouraged me to write this book. After leaving the US Military, Joyce was my first and best employer when I joined her consulting firm in Seattle years ago. Joyce is gone now, but her legacy lives on in this book.

*"I must be able to say with sincerity that to see things differently is a
strength, not a weakness, in my relationship with others."*
- Joyce Kuntz

I thank Joyce's husband, Ed Kuntz, who turned out to be the man who brought me to Seattle from Kansas City, to start my incredible second career as an Executive Coach.

For my coaching career, I thank Tony Robbins, Bernard Haldane, Jack Bissell, Len Drew, Wayne McCullum, Bob Schrier, John Hurtig, and Bob Gerberg for their mentoring and coaching.

I thank my Nephew, Rob Chase, for creating the superb cover graphics and his sound advice along the way.

I thank my editors, Adriane Hesselbein, Terri Beard, Lance Revo, Dan Labin, Dennis Cavin, Bill O'Donnell, Andrew Potter, and Kevin Hughes, who did a great job helping me make this book more understandable and useful.

A special thanks to my two dear friends, partners, and co-authors, Lee Lacy and Jason Bowne, who continue to support me in this worthwhile effort.

For all those whose names are not found here, rest assured that you are not forgotten. Your legacy lives on in my heart and in this book because of your immeasurable contributions to my life. This book is for you.

And, finally, I thank my soul-mate and wife, *Diana*, for her love, encouragement, and understanding throughout this process.

When I count my blessings, I always count her twice.

ABOUT THE FOUNDER

"I expect to pass through this world but once; any good thing therefore that I can do, or any kindness that I can show to any fellow creature, let me do it now; let me not defer or neglect it, for I shall not pass this way again."
- Stephan Grelle

Ed Murphy considers himself lucky. From age 7, he knew what he wanted to be when he grew up. He wanted to be a Soldier. In 1964, four days after graduating from High School, he joined the US Army and found himself in Basic Training and Advanced Infantry Training at Fort Dix, New Jersey.

A year later, Ed became a Cadet at the United States Military Academy at West Point. In 1970, he graduated as a 2d Lieutenant headed to Airborne and Ranger School, then off to Viet Nam for a year.

In 1978, Ed returned to West Point to teach Military Science and earned a Master's Degree from Long Island University in night school. His greatest achievement during his time in the military was helping 1400 soldiers begin their college education during his last two years in West Germany as a Battalion Commander. He wanted to give his soldiers something of real value - something that no one could ever take away. After 23 years as a US Army Officer, from Viet Nam to Desert Storm, he retired in 1993.

Ed then decided, with a little help from *Anthony Robbins*, that his second career would be as an Executive Coach. For the next 21 years, he worked for four of the largest consulting, outplacement and e-cruiting companies in America from Seattle, San Diego, to Kansas City.

In 2012, Ed retired a second time and decided to document everything he learned from those he admired and willingly followed over his 50+ years in both the US Military as an Army Officer and Corporate America as an Executive Coach.

Since many of them aren't alive today to tell their stories, he wanted to pay tribute to them before their lessons were lost forever. Thanks to them, he's collected thousands of small and simple things (tactics, techniques, and tools) that have helped and will continue to help future generations to maximize their true career potential by becoming more effective at work and in life.

In 2014, Ed created *TheCAREERMaker.com*, a site dedicated to providing the best-in-class wisdom, knowledge, and advice on how to maximize your true career potential by teaching three simple things; how to become absolutely essential and irreplaceable to any leader, how to become more effective tomorrow than you are today, and how to find and build the career you were meant to have. His greatest joy comes from helping others avoid or overcome the problems he faced during his lifetime.

In 2016, with the help of two partners and co-authors *Lee O. Lacy and Jason Bowne*, he finally completed *The Effectiveness Guide*, which teaches how to become more effective tomorrow than you are today by consistently producing excellent results; treating others with dignity, respect, and kindness; and helping others to do the same.

Today, Ed considers himself fortunate to get to live in Phoenix, AZ, where he enjoys writing, eating sushi, genealogy, and watching movies with family, friends, and his best friend and wife, *Diana*.

APPENDIX A:
GLOSSARY OF TERMS

After-Action Review (AAR): Professional discussion with all *Key Players* to focus on what happened vs. what was supposed to happen, and asks: "What did we learn that can make us better next time?"

Assignments *Accepted* and *Assigned:* Assignments received from your leader are called assignments *accepted.* From there, any assignments you make to others are called assignments *assigned.*

Band Of Excellence (or BOE): Set of performance (results and behavior) limits ranging from the Minimum (The Standard) - being the lower performance limit to the Maximum (The Goal) - being the upper performance limit. The difference between the Minimum Standard and the Maximum Goal is called the *Band of Excellence* for performance.

Brainstorming: Group process of identifying as many solutions/options to a specific problem without assessing, criticizing, or evaluating what is being said.

Competitive Advantage: Company has an attribute that allows it to outperform its competitors, like a special tax exemption.

Cross-Train: Technique of training each member how to perform the duties of at least two other members to minimize the effects of absenteeism.

Customer Focus Group: Group randomly selected to candidly assess products and services for usability, cost, variety, and complaints.

Dashboard: Display telling the current status of a project.

Frequently Asked Question (FAQ): A listing of the most Frequently Asked Questions (FAQ) and answers in the organization normally found on a shared-drive.

Follow through: Process of returning to the Delegator, either face-to-face or on the phone, and reporting the status of their request.

Flexibility to Respond: Leader's freedom of action to check on what's happening, to identify and resolve problems, to remain responsive to his leader, and to respond in case a Direct Report needs help.

Health and Welfare: Maintaining the stability, harmony, integrity, and cohesiveness of the team, while ensuring the standards for performance are maintained.

In-Charge: If you're *In-Charge*, it means *Take Charge!* Your leader is counting on you. Don't let him down. Your job is to plan, prepare, execute, and assess the project from start to finish. Be Proactive! See POC and *Take-Charge.*

In-Progress Review (IPR 1): First synchronization meeting with all *Key Players* to collaborate, coordinate, and achieve consensus on the project to ensure everything is on-schedule, everyone knows all changes, and no *Unresolved Issues* are remaining that could delay or stop the project. If so, project moves to Phase 2, Preparation.

In-Progress Review (IPR 2): Final synchronization meeting with all Key Players conducted 7-10 days before the start of the project to confirm all assigned tasks have been completed. If so, project moves to Phase 3, Execution.

Key Player: Anyone who must take action for a project to be a success. (could be Direct Report, peer, superior, or supplier)

Leadership Philosophy: Written document telling others your definition of leadership, your core values, what's important, what you stand for and what you won't stand for, your expectations of those you lead, what they can expect from you, and how you intend to lead those within your charge.

Plan of Action (POA): Effective POA must include Objective, Methods, Risk, Timetable, Resources Needed, and Unresolved Issues.

Positive Cash Flow (PCF): Used to measure profit through the combined effects of these components; increasing revenues, reducing operating costs, better use of available resources, and anticipating problems today to save money tomorrow

Preventive Actions: Actions planned 30-60-90 days in advance of a project's start, that are added to the project's timetable, to identify and resolve problems and mistakes to enhance project success.

Progress Briefing: Summary of work's progress giving the *Bottom line - Up front*, explaining the reasons, *Unresolved Issues*, and changes since the last report.

Staffing: Process of collaborating by circulating a document through all parties for their concurrence or non-concurrence with comments. In the end ask everyone, *"Can you follow, execute, and support this …? If not, why?"*

Standby: Assigned members available 24/7, with no other duties or responsibilities, to respond within minutes to needs of Project Lead, especially for unanticipated situations.

Unconscious Assumptions: Assumptions we make every day without thinking about it.

Unique Selling Proposition (USP): Marketing concept states that such campaigns made unique propositions to customers that convinced them to switch brands.

APPENDIX B:
TAKING "IMMEDIATE ACTION"

"I am only one, but still I am one. I cannot do everything, but still I can do something. And because I cannot do everything I will not refuse to do the something that I can do."
—Hellen Keller

When bad things happen, don't just sit there, do something! But, what? Effective people step up and take *Immediate Action*. *Immediate Action* is a drill used to react to unanticipated situations that could cause a work stoppage, property or equipment damage, a security breach, or physical injury. Here's an example of the steps of the *Immediate Action Drill:*

Assess the Situation: Either be *on-the-scene* or in communication with someone on the ground. Assess the situation based on the facts.

Notify emergency services (as needed) and your employer: If needed, notify Fire and Police, and call your employer to tell him what you know and what you have done.

Consider your Options: What should be done to stabilize the situation? What are your options? If time permits, collaborate with your team members/Key Players.

Select the Best Option: Select the best option or achieve consensus from your team members/Key Players.

Create a *Plan Of Action*: Create your *Plan of Action (Objective, Method, Risk, Timetable, Resources, and UIs).*

Take Decisive Action: *Take charge* and give new instructions to team members /Key Players. Supervise execution.

Reassess the Situation: What has changed? Did the situation stabilize or was the problem resolved?

If Yes, move to the final step.

If NO, repeat this process.

***Return and Report* to your employer:** Tell your employer what happened, what caused it, and what you recommend be done to ensure this never happens again.

Here's a great story:

Situation: *At 9 AM, two days before his company's annual Leadership Conference, Bob, the Project Lead, was conducting his final site inspection of the hotel venue and was astonished by what he saw. He tried to pull into the resort parking lot, which was blocked by construction vehicles that were tearing up the parking lot. This was a disaster for Bob because he had 150 Senior Executives driving and flying in from all over the country. Fortunately, Bob was trained in how to take Immediate Action.*

Step 1: *Bob didn't panic. He assessed the situation, took photos with his cell phone, spoke with the hotel manager, and learned that a major water main had broken and flooded the entire parking lot. Fortunately, the hotel still had water.*

Step 2: Call your employer: *At 9:30 AM, Bob called his leader and appraised him of the situation. There was no reason to call the Fire or Police department.*

Step 3: Consider your options: *At 10 AM, Bob called a meeting of all team members/Key Players at the company headquarters conference room to collaborate the best solution.*

Step 4: Select the Best Option: *Several people thought they needed to find another venue that could accommodate 150 people. They quickly discarded this option because they only had 48 hours. One person made the brilliant suggestion of renting a small fleet of shuttle vehicles to shuttle all participants from the airport and company headquarters to the hotel and back, 24/7. Consensus was achieved from all team members/Key Players.*

Step 5: Create a POA: *Together they created a Plan of Action to use shuttle vehicles to accomplish the objective.*

Step 6: Take Decisive Action: *Bob issued new instructions to all team members/Key Players and supervised all actions. He asked everyone to reconvene at 5 PM that day to share the status of their new assignments. All participants were informed of the situation and the shuttle vehicle solution.*

Step 7: Reassess the Situation: *At 5 PM that afternoon, Bob met with all team players/Key Players to ensure that everything was ready to move forward with a fleet of shuttle vehicles.*

Step 8: Return and Report to your employer: *At 6 PM, Bob called his leader and informed him that everything was ready for the conference. There was no reason to recommend what needed to be done to ensure this didn't happen again. The Leadership Conference went on without any further problems and turned out to be a great success.*

> *Bob looked defeat in the eye and refused to give up, snatching victory from the jaws of defeat.*

Can't you just DO NOTHIN?

Sure. But, doing nothing is a decision. You have this option every time you're faced with a problem. Do some problems sometimes correct themselves by doing nothing? Yes. Do some problems get worse by taking action, rather than doing nothing? Yes. Are there some problems that are better left alone? Sure. Just ask any *Fire-fighter*. Most of the time, all they can do is contain the fire and just let it burn itself out; let it *burn-to-the-ground*.

> *Doing nothing is making a decision by default.*

If you feel this is your Best choice, among all the choices you have available at the time, then do nothing – let it *burn-to-the-ground*. However, doing nothing and waiting are different decisions.

If you decide to wait, here are a few questions to ask:

- What are the adverse effects of not acting?
- How long do I have or what must happen (a decision point) before I'm forced to act?
- When is it too late for me to decide?
- How long after I decide, can action begin?
- What are all my options?
- What does my team recommend?

Have a *Contingency Plan (CONPLAN)* and the needed resources ready and prepositioned. Anticipate. Get ready!

APPENDIX C:
USING "PREVENTIVE ACTIONS"

This appendix assumes that you're the follower/Project Lead for an important project.

Preventive Actions are actions planned 30-90 days in advance of a project to identify and resolve problems early to enhance the success of a project.

Here are the most important *Preventive Actions* you can use to identify and resolve all the *Pre-Problems* (mistakes, defects, shortfalls, omissions, and errors) before they become problems.

THE PLANNING PHASE

Conduct Initial Site/Venue Inspection: Your first visit to the site to determine if it's suitable (available, accessible, amenities, cost, and sustainable) to support the project's requirements. Gather sufficient information (photos, dimensions, and sketch maps) to help select the best site/venue to create your Draft POA.

Create a Draft *Plan of Action* (POA): Your POA includes the Objective, Methods, Risk, Timetable, Resources Needed, and *Unresolved Issues (Appendix F)*.

Identify *Unresolved Issues*: Questions, Unknowns, Issues, Concerns, Shortfalls, Obstacles, Problems that could slow or stop your progress.

Conduct a *Risk Assessment*: With the help of your team, assess the physical, security, financial, and operational risk associated with the project and how they can be mitigated?

Identify the *Unintended Consequences & 2d/3d Order Effects*: Outcomes not expected by a decision/action and how the decision/action affects others.

Conduct a *Backbriefing*: Briefing you give to your leader, as to your *Plan of Action* (POA) to accomplish your leader's objective, to enhance mutual understanding and trust by an exchange of questions/answers to identify any unmet expectations/hidden surprises (*Appendix D*).

Provide *Advanced Warning*: Information you provide to all *Key Players* (anyone who must take action for the project to be a success) of what you're planning so they have as much time to plan as possible.

***Staff* the POA:** Your process of collaborating and achieving consensus by circulating a document (your POA) through all *Key Players* for their concurrence or non-concurrence with comments.

Conduct a *Decision Briefing*: Briefing you give to a Decision Maker (The *Bill Payer*), with all *Key Players* present, to obtain final approval, as needed.

Create *Contingency Plan*s: POA only executed in the event something bad happens that was anticipated like bad weather (*Appendix E*).

Conduct *In-Progress Review* (IPR 1): Your synchronization meeting with all *Key Players* to collaborate, coordinate, and achieve consensus on the project.

THE PREPARATION PHASE

Prepare to take *Immediate Action*: A disciplined drill used to react to unanticipated situations that could cause a work stoppage, property or equipment damage, a security breach, or physical injury (*Appendix B*).

Prepare an *Unanticipated Situation Plan*: POA that Includes *Priority Response System* (a cell phone protocol that permits you to contact *Key Players* quickly), *Pre-Stocking Site* (location of much-needed supplies), and *Quick Response Team* (on standing by with vehicles, cell phones, cash, and credit cards) .

Provide *Progress Briefings*: Your summary briefing to your leader telling the *actual progress* of your project in relation to the *planned progress* via presentation.

Provide *Situation Report*s: Verbal report to your leader telling him what you're working on, when you anticipate being done, and your *Unresolved Issues* and changes (*Chapter 7*).

Conduct a Final Site/Venue Inspection: Your last visit to the venue to determine if anything has changed since your initial inspection.

Conduct *In-Progress Review* (IPR 2): Your meeting conducted 7-10 days before the start of the project to confirm all assigned tasks have been completed on the date planned. If so, project moves to Phase 3, Execution.

THE EXECUTION PHASE

Conduct *Pre-Staging*: Involves the movement and storage of equipment and supplies to the site before the project, to make site set-up easier.

Conduct *Rehearsals*: Your last chance to see, practice, or test things before the project starts to help identify and correct mistakes in advance.

Conduct Site Set up: Conducted just before your project starts to configure the site as planned in POA. Having a site diagram (with extra copies) is a smart idea – showing where everything goes.

Project Starts: This is where you facilitate the actions of all *Key Players* to ensure the project achieves the desired objective. If problems occur, either execute *Immediate Action* (*Appendix B)* or execute the appropriate *Contingency Plan*, to keep the project moving forward.

Conduct Site Clearing: Time after the project to restore the site to its original configuration by removing equipment and supplies. Site may need to be cleared quickly to permit the next user to come in and stage their equipment.

THE ASSESSING PHASE

Assessing is a continuous process and is formalized during IPRs, *Situation Reports*, *Progress Briefings*, and an *After-Action Review*.

Conduct an *After-Action Review* (AAR): Your discussion with all Key Players to focus on what happened vs. what was supposed to happen, and asks: "What did we learn that can make us better next time?"

Conduct Project Close-out: Process of administering surveys, paying bills, sending letters, filing all supporting documents, and other final details.

<u>WARNING:</u>

If you fail to use these Preventive Actions when you plan any activity, do so at your own peril. You've been WARNED!

APPENDIX D:
GIVING AND RECEIVING "BACKBRIEFINGS"

"A leader is best when people barely know he exists, when his work is done, his aim fulfilled, they will say: we did it ourselves."
- Lao Tzu

Have you ever assigned a project to someone and wondered if he was planning to do what you expected him to do?

Here's one method of ensuring your expectations will be met; ask for a *Backbriefing*.

A Backbriefing is a briefing given by a Project Lead to his employer as to how he intends to accomplish the employer's objective.

Backbriefings enhance mutual understanding and trust by the exchange of questions and answers to ensure there are no unmet expectations or hidden surprises later.

What are the advantages of a Backbriefing?

- Facilitates a clear exchange of ideas, duties, and responsibilities to ensure the successful completion of a project

- Enhances communications, trust, confidence, and credibility

- Benefits all parties involved by reducing misunderstandings and confusion

- Gives the leader feedback to make corrections or give clarification as soon as he identifies any misunderstandings

When should a Backbriefing be Conducted?

- As the employer, request a *Backbriefing* either a few days after you assigned a new project or change, or 90 days prior to an expected project (already part of their job description like an annual trade show or recruiting event).

- As a Project Lead (PL), give a *Backbriefing* to your employer, as soon as possible, for all requested or expected projects or changes even if you do not need approval, to ensure there are no hidden surprises or expectations.

During a Backbriefing the employer should:

- Ask questions to uncover any misunderstandings

- Ensure the PL has a clear picture of the objective, its importance, and how it will be assessed

- Resist the urge to change the Method (How)

- Give encouragement, recognition, and support

During a Backbriefing the Project Lead should:

- Use the *Plan of Action* (POA) format to brief your employer (*Appendix F*).

- Capture all *Unresolved Issues* raised by your employer. Then, make changes to POA, as requested *(Appendix F)*.

- *Follow through* on questions you could not answer during the *Backbriefing*

- Obtain agreement on the desired end-results or Objective, how it will be measured, all major tasks to be completed, who should perform each task (*Key Player*), and the limit of your authority to make decisions and spend money

Note: If your employer doesn't want a Backbriefing, send him a copy of your draft POA.

APPENDIX E:
CREATING "CONTINGENCY/MITIGATION PLANS"

All you need is the plan, the roadmap, and the
courage to press on to your destination. "
- Earl Nightingale

A *Contingency Plan* is a POA only executed if something bad happens that you anticipated. Have you ever presented a POA to a *Decision-Maker*, only to have him ask, "Well, I like your plan, but what're we going to do if <u>this</u> happens?"

Effective people anticipate these questions and have *Contingency Plans* (or CONPLANS) ready to execute in the event <u>this</u> happens. These plans are only executed in the event <u>this</u> happens. Being prepared is the key! What's your plan?

Let's assume you're responsible for a major project, here's a *Risk Matrix* you could use to help you:

Anticipated Risk Matrix			
Bad Situation	*Impact*	*Probability*	*Action*
Inclement weather	Significant	Low	CONPLAN A
VIPs arrive late	Moderate	Medium	CONPLAN B
Lost baggage	Minor	High	CONPLAN C

There are two types of risk, *anticipated* and *unanticipated*. When it comes to *Anticipated Bad Situation (ABS)*, there are two critical things you must consider.

The first is *Impact* which means the effect on your project and is categorized as Significant, Moderate, or Minor. Based on your assessment, if this *ABS* happens, how will it impact/effect your project?

The second is *Probability* which means how likely is it that this *ABS* will happen and is categorized as High, Medium, or Low. Based on your assessment, how probable/likely is this *ABS* to occur. Obviously, if you have an *ABS* that has a *Significant* Impact and a *High* Probability of occurring, you'll need lots of help.

With the help of others, *Brainstorm* all the things that could *reasonably-go-wrong* that could stop or slow your project. Then, create a CONPLAN to mitigate their effect. You can't control everything that happens, but you can control your degree of planning, preparation and how you respond to the changing situation.

What's a Mitigation Plan?

A *Mitigation Plan* is a POA designed to get a project back *on track* by consolidating, and/or rescheduling certain tasks to finish on/or close to the originally planned date. No one likes being on a project when things are going badly. So, how can you get back *on track*?

The most important questions to ask if you ever have a Project in trouble:

- Can any tasks be eliminated, combined, or compressed?

- Any *Slack Time* in Preparation/Execution Phases?

- Can anything be done simultaneously (or done off-line and added later)?

- Do you need more people? Can overtime help?

- Should you go to a second shift or run 24-hours?

- Can working weekends and holidays help?

- Can the scope (requirements, complexity, goals) be reduced?

- Can the finish time be moved a few days to allow a successful completion?

Slack time: The amount of time in a schedule that a task can be delayed without causing a delay to other tasks or to the project's completion date. Note: It often takes twice as long as you think to get things done.

For those of you who think you'll never have to create a *Mitigation Plan* in your lifetime, think again. If you have a plan for getting your college education, MBA, or a Ph.D., what happens if you must take a year off? It's called a *Mitigation Plan* to help you pick up the pieces and move forward.

APPENDIX F:
CREATING A "PLAN OF ACTION" (POA)

"Plan for the future, because that is where you
are going to spend the rest of your life."
- Mark Twain

Any good *Plan Of Action* (POA) format has six components: Objective, Method, Risk, Timetable, Resources needed, and *Unresolved Issues*. When creating a draft POA, use this format and begin by adding everything you know for certain.

If you don't know a certain piece of information, still list the category, but show a TBA (To Be Announced) or a TBD (To Be Determined). For example, if you don't know the end time of an activity, show, End time: TBD. Practicing effective delegation allows the leader the time to do their primary job - to PLAN.

Effective Leader are not doers – they're Planners, Trainers,
Solution Providers, and Cheerleaders.

Planning is one of the most important factors that determines your ultimate success. When it comes to planning, you have two choices – either plan ahead or just hope for the best. Planning simply outlines a course of action to achieve a desired result.

Effective leaders focus on where they want their unit to be in the future. They develop plans (a roadmap) outlining how this journey will unfold. Their plans set unit goals and priorities to get there. They delegate assignments to their team members. Then, they supervise and *Follow through (Chapter 7)* on progress periodically.

Did you ever plan something and struggled trying to put everything together, so it made sense? Having a good *Plan of Action* (POA) format will help you overcome that problem. If you're looking for a good *Checklist* to use when creating your next POA, try this one:

OBJECTIVE:

- What's my access to sources of information?
- Who's this project for, where is this project
- Why is this being done? (Purpose)
- How important is this project and to whom is it important?
- What's the requirement? What is the scope (complexity) of work?
- Limit of my authority (decisions, delegate, spend $, hire and fire)?
- Is this approved by someone with authority?
- When is this project (Date/Times/Deadline)?
- How will success be measured and who will measure it?
- What's the most important task for this project to be a success?
- What must be ordered or started now?

METHODS:

- How should we do it? What are our options, and which is best?
- What're all the tasks involved and who's responsible to perform each task (*Key Player*)?
- What are the time phases and what happens during each phase?
- What must be done before, during and after the project?
- What specific instructions do we have for those delegated a task?
- How many people are expected to attend or are affected by this?
- What're our restrictions (can't do) and imperatives (must do)?
- Who has done this kind of project before?
- How'll this project be advertised or promoted?
- What are my Responsibilities, Expectations, Duties, Constraints, Authority, Projects, and Standards?
- Who're the most important people to talk to right now?
- What're the consequences if this turns out unsuccessful?

RISK:

*Physical: (Safety: Injury, Illness, or Death)

- ✓ What could cause or result in injury, illness, or death to anyone?

- ✓ Have we inspected the venue and what could cause or result in injury, illness, or death?

- ✓ Have we reviewed the checklist, *BY NOT FORGITIN NOTHIN*, to determine if we left anything out? (*Appendix G*)

- **Security: (Cyber & Property)**

  - ✓ What could cause or result in a cybersecurity breach, loss of sensitive/personal info, loss of intellectual property, or disruption of services?

  - ✓ What could cause or result in property damage or loss?

- **Financial:**

  - ✓ What could cause or result in either a financial loss?

  - ✓ What insurance protection do we need and is it *in-force?*

- **Operational:**

  - ✓ What could slow or stop this project?

  - ✓ What do we hope is true/necessary for this project to work?

  - ✓ What assumptions are needed to move the work forward?

  - ✓ If our assumption is false, what's our *Contingency Plan*? (*Appendix E*)

  - ✓ What are our *Unconscious Assumptions*? (*Appendix A*)

  - ✓ What are we forgetting to do? (*Appendix G*)

  - ✓ What are the *Consequences and Effects*? (*Appendix H*)

  - ✓ What *Preventive Actions* do I need to add to my POA to identify any *Pre-problems?* (*Appendix C*)

---

*Effective leaders are always present at the place and time of greatest danger or risk ready to take *Immediate Action (Appendix B)* in the event something goes wrong.

TIMETABLE:

- Planning backward from today, when are the Planning, Preparing, Executing and Assessment Phases?

- What's the *Project Briefing* schedule?

- When's the *Backbriefing* and start-time and end-time of the project?

- Which tasks and *Preventive Actions* must be done during each phase of the project?

- How long will each task take and what's the best sequence of these tasks and *Preventive Actions*?

- Which tasks can't start or finish without another task starting/finishing? (Dependent tasks)

- Which task needs to be started right now?

- What's the detailed schedule/program/calendar (enclosure)?

- When is the rehearsal and what will be rehearsed?

- Before the start: What do I want to see and when do I want to see it?

- Where can we add *Slack time into the Timetable just in case we need it?

Slack time: The amount of time in a schedule that a task can be delayed without causing a delay to other tasks or to the project's completion date.

Note: *Murphy's Law* says that it takes twice as long as you think to get things done.

RESOURCES NEEDED:

- What resources are most important for the success of this project?

- Who is paying for this and what must be ordered now?

- How much of each resource is needed, when and where?

- What skills, attitudes and/or knowledge are needed?

- Who has the skills we need?

- What people/groups have already conducted this project?

- When's the No-Later-Than (NLT) time we need these resources delivered?

- Who's responsible to provide the resources we need?

- Are there any special needs for safety, security, or those with disabilities?

- What're our *Shortfalls*?

- How much money can I spend? What's the Budget? Who pays?

Shortfall: Anything you need for completion of a project that you do not have, nor expect to have, when needed.

UNRESOLVED ISSUES:

- What do we need to know, but don't?

- What do we need, but don't have?

- What do we know for sure, but the answer is unsatisfactory or unacceptable?

- Who did this project last time and what problems did he encounter?

- What are the Questions, Unknowns, Concerns, Shortfalls, Obstacles, and Problems that could stop or delay our progress?

APPENDIX G:
DON'T FORGET NOTHIN!

Don't Forget Nothin!
Rogers' Rangers Standing Orders
By Major Robert Rogers, 1759

Have you ever created a POA, but later found that you forgot or left something out? Effective people have a checklist of all the things they need to consider?

Here's the start of a checklist to use during your lifetime to help you better prepare for anything.

- **Communications:** Do you have direct communication with your *Key Players* (anyone who must take action for the project to be a success) via cell phone or 2-way radios with back up batteries and chargers? Does everyone have a list of each other's phone numbers? What if they're not near their cell phone when you call (or are on another call)?

- **Fun:** Laughter, humor, music, breaks, snacks, games, awards, recognition, surprises, and prizes.

- **Getting attendees involved:** How can you put attendees to work? Have them physically do something, simulations, problem-solving, breakout sessions, circuit training, seminars, workshops, round-robin stations, role-playing, practical exercises, competition, or small group discussions.

- **Headquarters:** Is there a defined/known location at the event/activity, with a dedicated phone number, that is open 24/7 that tracks attendance, safety, first aid: with vehicle, driver, and map to the nearest hospital?

- **Life Support:** How will the participants be physically sustained (includes food, drink, snacks, ice, communications, lodging (if overnight), transportation, hygiene, toilets, electricity, cooking, refrigeration, liability insurance, sanitation (hand sanitizer, toilet paper), overhead shelter (if it rains), trash containers, and trash collection and removal). The longer the time and distance from home base, the more complicated the life support becomes.

- **Pre-work:** Do you want the participants to do something before the event and bring it with them? Do they need to review a *read-ahead packet*? If so, provide it in advance.

- **Program Support:** Audio/visual aids, handouts, loud-speaker, music, surveys, or backup generators?

- **Promotion:** How can you best advertise the event/activity that creates interest and anticipation? What's in it for them? What would make most people want to participate/attend? How will you communicate this to all invitees?

- **Quality Control (Assessment):** IPRs, AARs, meetings, deliverables, accountability, surveys, Contingency and Mitigation Plans, *Progress Briefings*, metrics, milestones, Timetables, and/or achieving consensus?

- **Rehearsals:** What do you need to see before you start? Do you need to practice, preview, or rehearse anything before the event/activity? Who is reviewing any documents, correspondence, etc. to see if they make sense and are correct?

- **Safety/Medical:** What if someone gets hurt? Do you need first aid kits, defibrillators, life jackets (if around water), and fire extinguishers? Are there any other hazards (like holes, cliffs, water, or any other way people could get hurt)? How can you mitigate this risk? Do you need members trained in CPR and first aid? How about Bee stings (EpiPen® need a prescription), bug spray, location of nearest hospital, vehicle designated to transport, maps to hospital, cell phones with 911 capabilities, and/or ambulance needed on the site?

- **Schedule/Program:** Is there ample time built into the program for all to have fun and do something meaningful, instead of just sitting there? How about a mixer (with name tags) so members can get to meet and know each other?

- **Search Plan:** What happens when someone is reported "missing," especially if away from the organization's property?

- **Security:** Are chaperones, guards, police, crowd and traffic control, or checkers needed? Cell phones (with chargers/extra batteries), cameras, and phone# available? Metal detectors needed to check for weapons?

- **Site Transition:** Site problems also include the poor scheduling of other units before and after your scheduled time. The concern here is that the previous unit may not be cleared of the site before you try to set-up. And, this includes your departure at the end of your project, before the next unit attempts to move in. Additionally, many units try to pre-stage and move supplies and equipment in the night before the project. Make sure you know who'll be there prior to you, and who is coming in after you to ensure the handoff is smooth.

- **Small Children:** Children are a special challenge because they're so mobile and seem to find their way, unsupervised, into places where they could potentially get hurt. If there's water, you'll need life vests, lifeguards and the like. If there's fire or anything hot, or vehicle traffic, or wells, or cliffs...get the idea?

- **Time:** When's the start time and end time? What else is going on around the selected site during this time? What else is going on in the lives of those assigned to perform certain projects/tasks like graduations, summer vacations, or the Super Bowl? Hint? What happened last year at the same time and place? What's your *Contingency Plan*?

- **Other:** Parking, access for delivery vehicles, traffic flow, who tracks who's there and who's not? Do you have a backup location in case of bad weather? Did you delegate all these tasks? Do you have consensus from all *Key Players*?

Note: You may not need all these reminders for your next project, but it's a nice checklist to add to your toolbox.

What are you forgetting to do?

Murphy's 5th Corollary:

**Whatever you start out to do, there will always
be something you should have done first.**

APPENDIX H:
ASSESSING YOUR "CONSEQUENCES AND EFFECTS"

"There are no rewards or punishments - only consequences."
- William Ralph Inge

If you intend to remain successful and effective over the long-term, you need to get really good at anticipating the *Unintended Consequences* and the *2d & 3d Order Effects* of your decisions.

Never begin something until you've assessed the consequences and effects of how it will end.

Most people fail to assess the consequences and effects of every choice/decision made to their project, whether they made it or not. It doesn't matter. Every decision has consequences and effects, sometimes good, sometimes-not so much.

The Project Lead's job is to anticipate the consequences and effects of every decision made to their project - before the decision is made!

Unintended Consequences are outcomes that aren't the outcomes expected by an action and are grouped into two categories:

- A *Positive*, unexpected benefit (usually referred to as serendipity or a windfall).

- A *Negative*, unexpected problem occurring in addition to the desired effect of the decision (while irrigation gives water for agriculture, it can also increase waterborne diseases). *Blowback* and *fallout* (what others might say and do) should also be considered.

2d and 3d Order Effects focus on how the decision affects others. Because some decisions can have wide-ranging effects, be sensitive to how your decisions affect others. Predicting *2d and 3d Order Effects* may result in finding resource requirements and changes to structures and procedures.

For example, when the CFO approves a change in vendors and suppliers, the consequences could be wide-ranging like:

- *2d Order Effects* may mean different ordering procedures and longer time delays
- *3d Order Effects* may need training on new ordering procedures and accountability

Keep asking; Then, what? / What's next? / What're we forgetting? / What will happen or what will we need to do in 30, 60, and 90+ days? Now you're ready to make your decision.

You're responsible for anticipating the consequences and effects of your decisions. Make sure you and your team think through all the consequences and effects before you make your decision.

OTHER BOOKS

THESE BOOKS WILL TEACH YOU HOW TO MAXIMIZE YOUR
TRUE CAREER POTENTIAL AND ARE AVAILABLE FROM
ALL MAJOR ONLINE BOOK RETAILERS

If you liked this book, you'll really like the others in our collection.

From *The Effectiveness Guide* series, topics include:

VOLUME 1: YOUR GUIDE TO BETTER FOLLOWERSHIP

CHAPTER 1: BY UNDERSTANDING FOLLOWERSHIP
CHAPTER 2: BY KNOWING YOUR "REDCAPS" COLD!
CHAPTER 3: WHAT'S MOST IMPORTANT TO YOUR EMPLOYER?
CHAPTER 4: BY "ADDING-VALUE" TO YOUR EMPLOYER
CHAPTER 5: BY BEING ACCOUNTABLE TO YOUR EMPLOYER
CHAPTER 6: BY CONTRIBUTING TO EMPLOYER MEETINGS
CHAPTER 7: BY FOLLOW UP & FOLLOW THROUGH
CHAPTER 8: BY BEING PROACTIVE
CHAPTER 9: BY GIVING "SITUATION REPORTS"
CHAPTER 10: BY ACCEPTING NEW ASSIGNMENTS
CHAPTER 11: BY AVOIDING THE REASONS PROJECTS FAIL
CHAPTER 12: BY CONDUCTING PROJECTS
CHAPTER 13: BY GIVING FEEDBACK TO YOUR EMPLOYER
CHAPTER 14: BY ENHANCING YOUR CREDIBILITY
CHAPTER 15: BY SUPPORTING YOUR EMPLOYER

APPENDIX A: GLOSSARY OF TERMS
APPENDIX B: TAKING "IMMEDIATE ACTION"
APPENDIX C: USING "PREVENTIVE ACTIONS"
APPENDIX D: GIVING AND RECEIVING "BACKBRIEFINGS"
APPENDIX E: CREATING "CONTINGENCY/MITIGATION PLANS"
APPENDIX F: CREATING A "PLAN OF ACTION"
APPENDIX G: DON'T FORGET NOTHIN!
APPENDIX H: ASSESSING "CONSEQUENCES AND EFFECTS"

VOLUME 2: YOUR GUIDE TO BETTER DELEGATING

VOLUME 3: YOUR GUIDE TO BETTER PLANNING

VOLUME 4: YOUR GUIDE TO BETTER ORGANIZING

VOLUME 5: YOUR GUIDE TO BETTER COMMUNICATING

VOLUME 6: YOUR GUIDE TO BETTER PROBLEM-SOLVING

CHAPTER 1: BY KNOWING HOW PROBLEMS ARE RESOLVED

CHAPTER 2: BY FINDING THE CAUSE OF PROBLEMS

CHAPTER 3: BY GATHERING RELEVANT INFORMATION

CHAPTER 4: BY FINDING ALL POSSIBLE SOLUTIONS

CHAPTER 5: BY TESTING POSSIBLE SOLUTIONS

CHAPTER 6: BY SELECTING THE BEST SOLUTION

CHAPTER 7: BY PREVENTING PROBLEMS

CHAPTER 8: BY CORRECTING PROBLEMS

CHAPTER 9: BY ELEVATING PROBLEMS YOU CAN'T RESOLVE

CHAPTER 10: BY MAKING BETTER DECISIONS

CHAPTER 11: BY USING DECISION-MAKING TOOLS

CHAPTER 12: BY HELPING YOUR LEADER DECIDE

CHAPTER 13: BY OVERCOMING DECISION-MAKING OBSTACLES

CHAPTER 14: BY ANTICIPATING & EMBRACING CHANGE

CHAPTER 15: BY DEALING WITH AMBIGUITY

CHAPTER 16: BY USING CHANGE CONTROL PROCEDURES

CHAPTER 17: BY MAKING CHANGES TO YOUR PROJECT

CHAPTER 18: BY CONDUCTING REHEARSALS

APPENDIX A: GLOSSARY OF TERMS

APPENDIX B: REAL WORLD PROBLEM-SOLVING EXAMPLE

APPENDIX C: ADVANCE PROBLEM-SOLVING WITH VUCA

APPENDIX D: DON'T FORGIT NOTHIN!

VOLUME 7: YOUR GUIDE TO BETTER AWARENESS

VOLUME 8: YOUR GUIDE TO BETTER TRAINING

VOLUME 10: YOUR GUIDE TO BETTER CHARACTER

CHAPTER 1: BY KNOWING THE POWER OF CHARACTER

CHAPTER 2: BY RECOGNIZING THE SIGNS OF MATURITY

CHAPTER 3: BY IDENTIFYING RIGHT FROM WRONG BEHAVIOR

CHAPTER 4: BY KNOWING HOW CHARACTER IS LEARNED

CHAPTER 5: BY "CELEBRATING THE STRUGGLE"

CHAPTER 6: BY CHOOSING GOOD ROLE MODELS

CHAPTER 7: BY PROTECTING YOUR CHARACTER

CHAPTER 8: BY RECOGNIZING YOUR LIMITING BEHAVIORS

CHAPTER 9: BY BECOMING MORE SELF-AWARE

CHAPTER 10: BY BECOMING MORE "INTERDEPENDENT"

CHAPTER 11: BY BECOMING MORE RESILIENT

CHAPTER 12: BY DEMONSTRATING "MORAL COURAGE"

CHAPTER 13: BY BEING HUMBLE

CHAPTER 14: BY PROTECTING THEIR "HEALTH & WELFARE"

CHAPTER 15: BY LIVING YOUR " LEADERSHIP PHILOSOPHY"

CHAPTER 16: BY SERVING YOUR TEAM

CHAPTER 17:   BY TREATING OTHERS WITH "DIGNITY, RESPECT, AND KINDNESS"

THE EFFECTIVENESS GUIDE (INCLUDES VOLUMES 1-10)

All the above books are also available from our Book Store at ***TheEffectivenessGuide.com***.

From *TheCareerMaker.com series*, topics include:

- Choosing a Career That Matters

- Interview Like You Mean It

- Does Your Resume Make Your Phone Ring?

- Negotiating Total Compensation

- 19+ Proven Ways to Get Your Resume to the Right People

- Changing Your Career?

- Getting THE Call for Job Interviews and Offers

All the above books are also available from our Book Store at *TheCareerMaker.com.*

NOTES

None

ONE LAST THING...

Finally, if you feel this information could help someone else, please take a few moments to let them know. If it turns out to make a difference in their life, they'll be forever grateful to you – as will I.

Let's make a difference together – one person at a time!

All the best!

Ed

Founder of *TheEffectivenessGuide.com*
Coauthor of *The Effectiveness Guide*
email: ed.murphy77@gmail.com

Stop wishing you were better and do something about it today!

WANT TO STAND OUT?

See How at
TheEffectivenessGuide.com

INDEX

Made in the USA
Lexington, KY
28 April 2019